Frederic William Farrar

General Aims Of The Teacher

Frederic William Farrar

General Aims Of The Teacher

ISBN/EAN: 9783741183560

Manufactured in Europe, USA, Canada, Australia, Japa

Cover: Foto ©Thomas Meinert / pixelio.de

Manufactured and distributed by brebook publishing software
(www.brebook.com)

Frederic William Farrar

General Aims Of The Teacher

𝔓itt 𝔓ress 𝔖eries.

GENERAL AIMS OF THE TEACHER,

AND

FORM MANAGEMENT.

TWO LECTURES

DELIVERED IN THE UNIVERSITY OF CAMBRIDGE
IN THE LENT TERM, 1883,

BY

F. W. FARRAR, D.D.

ARCHDEACON OF WESTMINSTER,

AND

R. B. POOLE, B.D.

HEAD MASTER OF BEDFORD MODERN SCHOOL.

𝖢ambridge :

AT THE UNIVERSITY PRESS.

𝕷ondon : . C. J. CLAY, M.A. & SON,
CAMBRIDGE UNIVERSITY PRESS WAREHOUSE,
17, PATERNOSTER ROW.

1883

THE Lectures contained in this volume are of a similar character to those published by the Cambridge University Press at the beginning of the present year. It is hoped that their appearance in a permanent form may be a welcome contribution to the literature of the Science of Education.

OSCAR BROWNING.

KING'S COLLEGE, CAMBRIDGE,
May, 1883.

CONTENTS.

GENERAL AIMS OF THE TEACHER.

By CANON FARRAR.

.

GENERAL AIMS OF THE TEACHER[1].

IF this were meant to be a formal lecture before the University, I might well shrink from it, for I have only had a few short fragments of overburdened time to give to it. But I assume throughout that I am speaking only—and speaking, I might almost say, confidentially—to a small body of young men, who intend to devote their lives to the honourable labours of the teacher. I have no claim to address you, even thus familiarly and unreservedly, beyond the fact that I was invited to do so. I shall not pretend to speak *ex cathedrâ*, or as though by any work of mine I had earned the smallest right to dogmatize; but I might almost begin in the words with which Quintilian begins his "Institutio Oratoria," "Post impetratam studiis meis quietem, quae per viginti annos erudiendis juvenibus impenderam." I should, indeed, have to alter the word *quietem;* for leisure is a thing to which I have bidden a final farewell. But, for twenty years—for twenty years happier than I can hope to see again—I enjoyed the high honour of being first an Assistant-master, and then a Head-master, in great English Public Schools. During that time hundreds of boys have passed under my hands, so

[1] A lecture delivered at Cambridge, March 3, 1883, under the direction of the Teachers' Training Syndicate.

1—2

that I have had a large share in the training of young
Englishmen of every age, and of every degree of capacity.
When first I left Cambridge, not only before I became a
Fellow, but even before the Tripos List was out, I was
invited to this work by the offer, from Bishop Cotton, of a
Mastership at Marlborough College.   I had not been much
more than a year at work—sharing the teaching of the Sixth
Form with the Head-master—when I was invited to Harrow
by Dr Vaughan.   There I laboured for fifteen years.   At the
end of that time I was elected to the Mastership of Marlborough, and, after nearly six years of ruling a prosperous
and happy Public School, I was taken, sorely against my
will, to other work, not only of yet deeper anxiety and
severer strain, but with none of the sunshine and brightness
of the life which, up to that time, God had granted to me.
I love, I honour the work of a schoolmaster.   I say with
Luther, "If God had not sent me to be a preacher of His
word, I should choose, before all things, to be a schoolmaster."   If, then, you find my advice homely and commonplace, as indeed it will be, I will ask you to bear with it as
being, at any rate, the fruit of genuine experience.   That
which is not new may yet, perhaps, acquire a certain novelty
and a certain worth, when it represents a fragment of the
hard earnings of living experience.   In the now distant days
when I left Cambridge as a youth, no one ever dreamed of
training teachers.   The art of teaching was supposed to
spring into full-born life,—often, I fear, not until the head
of the teacher had been cleft in twain in more ways than
one.   I do not think that one word had ever been said to
me about boys, or the best method of teaching them, or the
wisest plans for rendering those methods effective, when, at
the age of twenty-two, I first took my seat in the Master's

chair. *Experientia docet*—"Experience," to repeat the venerable joke of my old Cambridge tutor, "does it." To the teacher, as to all others, experience is the best, if also the sternest, of all instructors; and no one can supersede the necessity for her often painful lessons. But the *pain* of *some*, at least, of her lessons she does not grudge to remit to those who are humble enough to learn from others, and not to despise the application of truths because they are known to be so very true.

I. When any of you find yourselves in the position which fell to my lot thirty years ago—the position of being suddenly set down to teach a large form of boys, some of whom are only a few years younger than yourselves; boys inclined to fun, perhaps even to mischief, perhaps even to turbulence,—almost the first qualification which I should postulate, would be *a sense of the importance, the dignity, the sacredness of your task.* If a teacher is wholly unimpressed by the sense of this sacredness,—an impression which may remain with him, not as a burden, but as an inspiration even in his lightest hours,—I do not think that he will ever make a perfect teacher. The teacher's hand must always be on the tiller, but, if he would steer aright, his eye must ever be on the directing star. His task is sacred, for two reasons:— one, the transcendent importance of the results which it produces; the other, the rapidity and intensity of the influences which tend to those results.

1. When the great scholar Muretus was travelling in the disguise of a beggar, he was taken ill at a foreign town. His illness called for some serious operation; and, talking to each other in Latin, the physicians said, "Fiat experimentum

in corpore vili." "Vilemne animam appellas" exclaimed the indignant scholar to his startled hearers, "pro qua Christus non est dedignatus mori?" The anecdote tells us why every soul of every child of man is to the Christian sacred, and even of infinite sacredness. But, quite apart from this thought, the vast possibilities which lie in every human soul, should be enough to make the task of its training a solemn and a sacred one. In 1793, when he was expecting every hour to be led off to the guillotine, Dupont de Nemours said,—"Even at this incomprehensible moment, when morality, enlightenment, love of country, all of them only make death at the prison door, or on the scaffold, more certain,—yes, on the fatal tumbril itself,—with nothing free but my voice, I could still cry '*Take care,*' to a child that should come too near the wheel. Perhaps I may save his life; perhaps he may, one day, save his country." But I think that religious men—men who not only believe in God, but have faith in Him—must feel this more deeply than others, even as religious *nations* have so felt it. Contrast the neglect of early education and the contempt in which teachers were held among the Greeks and Romans—a neglect and contempt so feelingly portrayed by Juvenal—with the feelings of the Jews, as shown in many passages of the Talmud. In one of these, they tell how once, in a great drought, their greatest Rabbis prayed and wept for rain, and the rain came not. And, at last, a common-looking person got up and prayed to Him who causeth the wind to blow and the rain to descend, and instantly the heavens began to cover themselves with clouds, and the rain began to fall. "Who art thou," they cried, "whose prayers have alone prevailed?" And he answered, "I am a teacher of little children." Who shall estimate what the world has gained by wise education, and what it has lost by the neglect of it? "Providence," as Victor Hugo says, "entrusts us with a portion of its own functions. God says to man, I confide to thee this child." "All," says Dr Arnold, "who have meditated on the art of governing mankind, have felt that the fate of empires depended on the education of youth." "Give me the children," said Cardinal Wiseman, "and in twenty years all England shall be Catholic." "Train a boy well or ill, and of the effects of your training," said Sydney Smith, "you can neither measure the quantity nor perceive the end. It may be communicated to children's children; it may last for centuries; it may be communicated to innumerable individuals." Among the busts of the Roman Emperors at the British Museum, you may see one of a child about six years old. It would be impossible to find a face of more exquisite and winning loveliness. The hair rests in sunny waves about a smooth forehead; the features are full of mirthful innocence. You wish to see what sort of a man that child became. You anticipate a face full of manly beauty. What you see is a face puffed, bloated, sullen, of which you know not whether it repels you most by its brutal sensuousness, or by its sanguinary ferocity. Who had the training of that bright and trustful child? First, a barber and a dancer; then relatives and parents of exceptional infamy. He was the wild beast of the Apocalypse, the Emperor Nero. On the other hand, consider how many have borne testimony to the truth that a child trained in the way wherein he should go, will not depart from it; will not *wholly*, will not *finally* depart from it,—at the worst will not *so* wholly and *so* finally depart from it as if he had *not* been rightly trained. "I bless God heartily," said Lord Russell on the scaffold, "that I had the advantage of a religious education; for even when

I minded it least, it still hung about me and gave me checks."

2. Then, besides this vast importance of the effects he may produce, no wise and good teacher should ever forget the rapid intense impressions—often, alas! unconscious, unintended impressions—which, for good or for evil, he will inevitably produce. Every biography is full of the *little* things, the apparently infinitesimal trifles, which have guided or moulded human careers. We all know the story of King Alfred and the illuminated missal. Sir W. Jones attributed his learning to his mother's invariable answer to his questions, "Read and you will know." The first impulse which swayed the genius of Vauban, the great engineer of his age, was being shut up in a room which had nothing in it but a clock. "That picture," said Turner, pointing to a mezzotint of Vandervelde, which he had seen as a boy, "made me a painter." Mr Ruskin attributes his art impulses, in no small measure, to his tracing out the patterns of the carpet, when, as a little boy, he had no toys to amuse him. Darwin tells us how the engraving of a tropic scene in one of his books, as a child, ultimately culminated in his accompanying, as a naturalist, the voyage of the *Beagle.* When we visit Rugby, they show us Arnold's table, with the inscription on it, written by the present Archbishop of Canterbury, "In hâc sellâ Arnoldus literas docebat...Ad virtutis veritatisque amorem, Domini Jesu imitationem, voce, fronte, moribus suos excitabat." I remember, years ago, when Dr Benson, then a Rugby master, showed me the inscription, I told him that the word which struck me most was "*fronte.*" Arnold's very look, the look of a good as well as of a strong and resolute man, was an education to his pupils. For this reason

I am convinced that no *bad* man can ever be a good teacher.
Boys catch the very tones of their Head-masters, and, in
examining written answers, you may almost tell what school
a Sixth Form boy comes from, if you know his master's
handwriting. Teachers have a vaster power in their grasp
than any which they can imagine. Humboldt, on the banks
of the Orinoco, saw the naked copper-coloured children of
the Indians rubbing the shining seeds of the Negretia, and
amusing themselves by attracting straws and feathers with
them. How little did those Indian children guess, how
little did even the wisest ancients know, when they observed
the attractive powers of rubbed amber, and called it ἤλεκτρον,
that the force which they were eliciting was the same force
which crashes in the thunder, and flames in the lightning!
and yet that men should soon learn to seize it by its wing of
fire, and bid it carry their messages in a moment round the
girdled globe; or, with its wild spirit tamed to service of
commodity, should make their nightly cities as bright as day!
But what is the lightning to the spirit of man?

> "How swift is the glance of the mind !
>   Compared with the speed of its flight,
> The tempest itself lags behind,
>   And the swift-speeding arrows of light."

Understand it, train it, direct it rightly, and you shall send
it flashing through the generations, flashing over all the
world.

3. Now, in teaching and training, one of your first
requisites will be the power of Discipline. It is a curious
gift. You cannot by any means always predict who would,
or who would not, be likely to possess it. I have known
some teachers, very great and very eminent men, who were

wholly without it. One of these was my dear friend and
teacher, Frederic Denison Maurice. You could not meet a
truer man, or look on a nobler face. I had the great advantage of being for three years his pupil at King's College.
We all knew that he was a great man, an honoured man, a
deep thinker,—many of us longed to learn from him ; yet,
again and again, his lectures at King's College used to be
interrupted by childish and brainless disturbances, which
either would not have occurred at all, or could have been
instantly suppressed by many a graduate of the most commonplace attainments. Another great man wholly devoid
of powers of discipline, was my dear friend and fellow-
undergraduate, James Clerk Maxwell. His lectures, when
he did lecture to large promiscuous bodies of youths, were
often a mere bear-garden, in which he was helpless—strong
and great and good as he was—either to control or to teach.
The *special* gift of disciplinary power—such a gift as that
possessed by Pestalozzi, who once reduced to order a turbu-
lent throng of boys by simply lifting his finger—is very
rare ; the total absence of it is also very rare. It is a sort
of knack which may be acquired. When authority is firmly,
kindly, justly exercised—when the teacher is calm, and
without nervousness, and means both to rule and to teach—
when he shows from the first the "comitate condita gravitas,"
he does not often fail. Most men, after a little preliminary
experience, become at least moderate disciplinarians. When
I first went to Marlborough as an Assistant-master, in 1854,
one so utterly inexperienced, and so exceptionally ignorant
of boys, and of Public Schools, and indeed of the common-
est facts of life, as I was, might well have thought the task
very formidable. The school was in the detumescence of a
most ruinous rebellion. The first sight which caught my

eye was an inscription on the wall in chalk, in foot-long letters, "Bread or Blood." I was told a curious history of some of my boys :—how the temper of one was absolutely ungovernable; how another had recently bored a hole into a gas-pipe with a red-hot poker; how the windows of the common-room used, not long before, to be broken with stones; how, in one master's form, the boys used to catch mice and let them loose. Moreover, I was put to teach, as none of you will be, in a huge schoolroom, in which some six other large forms were being simultaneously taught. The circumstances were so distracting that, in one of my first letters to a Cambridge friend, I said, that to be a teacher one needed the voice of a Stentor, the hands of a Briareus, and the eyes of an Argus. But I soon found that, if a teacher have but the most moderate powers, he is effectually supported, not only by the natural and inherent good sense and right feeling of his scholars, but also by the routine, the discipline, and the traditions of a great school. I discovered in later days, that when, in a great English Public School, a Head-master turned his head, it was enough to reduce a noisy room to silence. The other day, the schoolroom of a certain great school, on a wintry morning, was a tempest of contagious coughs. Now, nothing is more difficult than to keep down coughing. The Head-master got disturbed; he simply said, in the quietest possible voice, "Less noise if you please; repress your coughing,"—and lo! not one cough was heard again till prayers were over. At Marlborough, as a very young Assistant-master, I had the quite inestimable blessing of a beautiful example. Surrounded by difficulties, in a school just out of rebellion, at that time badly fed, and not long before inadequately officered, so crushed with debt that almost the first thing

Bishop Cotton said to me was, "You know this school may disappear any day in blue smoke,"—I saw how, by patience, by humour, by tact, by wisdom, by goodness, by fearless courage, by firm inflexible justice, he became to that school a second founder, and a name and tradition of good for ever. In a moral and intellectual, if not in a physical sense, "lateritiam invenit, marmoream reliquit." It is needless to say that he was a good disciplinarian.

If, after a year's experience, a man cannot keep boys in perfect order, he will save himself much misery and much obstructiveness, if, as I have advised many a young graduate to do,—for his own sake, and still more for the sake of others—he will have the courage to choose another career.

4.   But I should give this advice, even more strongly, if a master can indeed keep discipline, but it is only the discipline of death; only a discipline maintained by constant punishments. Who can estimate the evil which has been done by centuries of flogging? I quite admit that many a rough nature, trained upon it, has not been much the worse for it. But, if you want to estimate the harm it has done, read De Quincey's Autobiography. As a young boy, I was trained under that system. I was certainly diligent, I was not exceptionally stupid; but yet I was for some time among those

"Si quos Orbilius ferulâ scuticâque cecidit."

For every mistake in the multiplication table—for every slip in an "Arnold's Exercise"—for every bad piece of construing,—the formula used to be, "Hold out your hand"; and there followed an excruciating blow across the tender part of the palm. In my early school days, I have, as an every-day matter, seen backs scored with red and blue weals, which, in these days, would secure, in favour of the most mischievous street Arab, a verdict in any police court. Down to times so recent has the pestilent practice of the *plagosus Orbilius* reigned supreme. They still show at Rome the birch of the saintly Gregory. I should like every schoolmaster to read the wise advice and reproof of St Anselm to the Abbot who complained that he never ceased beating the boys at his school day or night, and that they grew up dull and brutal. But the Saint's advice was not remembered. Longchamps, Bishop of Ely, in Richard I.'s time, used to prick his pages with an ox-goad. English literature, from Skelton, who tells us how his back was "scooryd" at school, and Piers Plowman, who says, "You mased the boye so sore with beatyng that he coulde not speake a worde,"—down to Pope, who talks of the birch blushing with patrician blood, and Coleridge, who describes the flagellations habitually inflicted by the Rev. J. Bowyer, and De Quincey, who tells how a brutal flogging drove forth his beautiful brother "Pink" a wanderer in the world,— English literature is full of this gross cruelty. Agnes Paston, in 1457, writes to Greenfield a request that, if her boy at Eton has not done well, "he will truly belash him." She beat her daughter once or twice a week, sometimes twice a day, and broke her head in two or three places. It is said that Lady Russell, daughter of Sir Antony Cook, beat her little son by a former marriage to death, for a blot on his copy-book. Every one knows the pathetic lines of Tusser:—

> "From Paul's I went, to Eton sent,
> To learn straightways the Latin phrase,
> Where fifty-three stripes given to me
> At once I had ;

For fault but small, or none at all,
It came to pass thus beat I was,
See Udall.I see the mercy of thee
To me poor lad!"

Every one knows how Lady Jane Grey describes the treatment which she received from her own parents, unless she did everything "so perfitely as God made the world." " I am so sharply taunted," she says, "so cruellie threatened, yea, presentlie sometimes with pinches, nippes, and bobbes, and other waies which I will not name,—so without measure misordered, that I think myself in hell[1]." Every one knows how a brutal pedagogue showed off his discipline to Erasmus, by calling up a boy, and shamefully beating him for nothing at all, and simply "pour encourager les autres." One is reminded by these quotations, of what Plautus wrote not far from two millenniums earlier :—

"Quum librum legeres, si una peccavisses sullaba,
Fieret corium tam maculosum quam'st nutricis pallium."

It is literally only in this generation that this reign of terror has wholly ceased. Even in Mr Bosworth Smith's *Life of Lord Lawrence,* we read that, when asked whether he had ever been flogged as a boy, the great Proconsul replied with grim satisfaction and Spartan brevity, "I was flogged every day of my life at school except one, and then I was flogged twice." If the Teachers' Syndicate had existed in old days, one hopes that such a system would long ago have received its death-blow. And here let me give my deliberate testimony, from six year's experience as Headmaster of a school of more than 580 boys, that well-trained

---

[1] For one or two of these references, I am indebted to Mr Furnival's *Early Education in England.*

English boys may be guided by a thread; and that, in a good English school, corporal punishment may be so much minimized as to be wholly exceptional, and in some of the best schools almost entirely unknown. Dr Busby and Dr Keate may doubtless, in their own way, have been great teachers, but let us hope that the barbarous methods in which they exulted, were *vitia temporum*, not *vitia hominum*, and that henceforth they are over for ever.

5. But I would apply the spirit of the remark much more widely. I would say, that in ordinary teaching, the more you punish in any way, the worse master you are; that he is the best master who needs to punish least; and that, if such a thing should exist as a perfect master, it is probable that, so far as mere teaching is concerned, he would never have to punish at all. "Impositions," "lessons to write out," "lines," "abstracts," whatever they are called, are, in the essence of them, confessions of weakness. They are in many respects injurious, and there is very little to be said for them. "Write me out five hundred lines of Homer, with all the accents." I have known masters say that, perhaps in a moment of anger, perhaps for no moral fault;—but, what a bad punishment! Scarcely ever will the good master have to resort to such a method. When a form sees that he is in earnest; that lessons *must* be learnt; that if they are neg- lected from idleness, they will have to be said again; where the master is endowed with such gifts, that he can encourage, help, sympathise, inspire,—he will either find punishments all but extinct, or he will measure by their frequency his own incapacity, and his own failure.

6. And I would still further apply the remark to abuse,

taunts, sarcasm. I have known masters who habitually shout at their boys, "little fool," "little idiot," "little ass," and so on. A master is very ill-advised to use such language; he cannot do it without great and serious loss of dignity. I have known a master upbraid a boy with stupidity. Now there is a *moral anaisthesia*—a dementation preceding doom —which may sometimes deserve such an epithet; although "hebetes et indociles pauci admodum; in pueris elucet spes plurimorum." But, if a boy be really and congenitally dull —dull, that is, in certain subjects, for a boy dull in all subjects is very rare—"falsa enim est querela paucissimis hominibus vim percipiendi quæ tradantur esse concessam,"—it is as shameful and useless a cruelty to taunt him with being stupid, as to taunt him, as Lord Byron's mother used her son, with a personal defect. A clever and quick master, worried by a heavy, obstinate boy, may be tempted to keen sarcasm. I hold that, except to suppress insolent vice—in which case sarcasm may be used as keen as a razor's edge— such sarcasm is an inexcusable tyranny. I once knew a boy, now in an important position, and an honoured and useful member of society, who somehow seemed to invite ridicule, partly by his absence of humour, partly by his peculiarities. Now Bishop Cotton had a singular fund of dry but inimitable humour, and one day he made the whole class laugh by his satirical criticisms of this boy. When the lesson was over, the boy waited, went up to the master, and said with quiet dignity,—"Sir, I am not clever; I dare say my work is very poor; but it is not my fault. I do my best, and I do not think it just that you should make me your laughing-stock." Cotton listened to him with kind sympathy, and—such is the characteristic mark of a good man—he was never once known to use his powers of sar-

casm in the same way again. I think it may help a master
to feel in how very deep a sense it is true, that "*maxima
debetur pueris reverentia*," if he will always steadily bear in
mind two thoughts—one, that every event of those days will
live for years in the vivid photograph of his pupils' memories;
the other, that, a year or two hence, he will meet those
pupils as bearded men, whom, if he has been unjust to
them or unkind, he will be unable to meet without a pang.

7. Then I would say, *Trust your boys.* Take their
word whenever it is possible; I would almost say, sometimes
when it seems impossible to do so. You will think that, if
I have not yet reached my dotage, I must be near it, being
in my anecdotage; but, as it is my sole and very humble
desire to be of use, I will tell you two incidents which
impressed me with the value of this lesson.

A few days after I went to Marlborough, I was in
charge, after dark, of a very large schoolroom full of boys,
of whom many belonged to the old *régime*. To keep order
among them all, quite unaided, was very far from an easy
task. Boys often liked to get out into the court. A boy
came up to me with his handkerchief at his nose, and said,
"Please, sir, may I go out?—my nose is bleeding." I am
sorry to say that I took away his hand. His nose *was*
bleeding, and, having had no special reason to suspect the
lad, I saw at once how wrongly I had done, and frankly
begged his pardon. Some years afterwards, at Harrow, two
boys brought me Latin exercises, marked at intervals by the
same grotesque mistakes. It seemed certain that those
exercises could not have been done independently. I ques-
tioned the boys. Both assured me that there had been no
copying. One, whom I had always considered to be a boy

of high *morale*, assured me of this again and again with passionate earnestness. I said to him,—"If I were to send up these two exercises to Dr Vaughan, if I were to show them to any jury in England, they would say that these resemblances could scarcely be accidental, except by something almost like a miracle. But you both tell me, and assure me, that you have not copied. I cannot believe you would lie to me; I must suppose that there has been some most extraordinary accident, of what nature I cannot tell. I shall say no more." Years after, one dark night as I returned from chapel,—it was so dark that I could not see the boy's face, but only recognise his voice,—that boy, who was then a monitor, and near the top of the school, said to me, "Sir, do you remember that exercise in the fourth form?" "Yes," I said, "I remember it well." "Well, sir, I told you a lie. It *was* copied. You believed me, and the remembrance of that lie has remained with me, and pained me ever since." That boy is now an able and distinguished man of letters. I am inclined to think that he was more effectually taught, and more effectually punished, than if I had refused to accept his protests, and had "sent him up for bad." But, while I am on this subject, I will add my conviction that, during twenty years, I was very seldom told a falsehood. One reason for this was, not only that I made it a general rule to believe a boy's word, but still more that I took extreme pains to avoid ever *surprising* a boy into a denial, or an equivocation. I believe that many falsehoods are—to quote Cardan's expression—manslaughters upon truth, not murders. They spring from the instinct of self-protection always shown by the timid animal. By a blundering method in this matter, it is fatally easy to entrap a boy—even a boy naturally truthful—not only into one lie, but into a series of

linked lies, such as shall injure his character, and rest like a
chain of fire upon his conscience, for many a long day—
nay, more, such as may involve a long course of self-decep-
tion, and fatally undermine his moral strength. If he
have been suddenly surprised, by being taken off his guard,
into *one* lie, the very shame of so unwonted an offence will
lead him into another, and yet another, that he may buttress
up the first. Trust your boys; teach them to trust you;
rely on their sense of your sympathy and kindness, and not
on fear; do not take them off their guard; say a few kind
words to a boy; give him time to think; arm him against
his own weakness; and you will rarely be told anything
which is not true.

8. Once more, I would say, "Do not be too niggardly
of praise and encouragement." I say this very earnestly.
When I came up to Trinity College, although I had won
scholarships and prizes elsewhere, I was, in many respects,
very ill-prepared, and I think that at least a score of men,
even in my own College, would very easily have beaten me.
It was, in a worldly point of view, very important to me to
do well in the Tripos. Great personal diffidence, added to
a temperament which was a very anxious one, weighed
heavily upon me. In my last Long Vacation, when time
was more than ever important, I caught what used to be
called the Cambridge fever. You know that praise and
encouragement have never been prominent parts in our
Cambridge system of teaching. For most men, perhaps,
they are not needed, but for some men they are; at any
rate, I am quite sure that, if any one had ever said to me,
"You need not be anxious, or distress yourself; you may
look forward with reasonable certainty to a first-class," he

would have lifted from my mind a load of heavy care. I
do not think that, when we have passed these ordeals, we
ever adequately recall the pressure which results to many
young minds from the ever-extending system of competition.
I recall how one man, now of the highest rank, once left
Cambridge suddenly in an agony of disappointment, after
failing to win a scholarship. I recollect the case of another,
who, though he became a Fellow, yet took to drinking as
the result of a comparative failure in the Tripos, and now
lies in a nameless grave. I think of a Marlborough boy, a
bright young lad, who went to Oxford, and on the very eve
of an examination was found dead, with a gun beside him, in
his own rooms. This *mandarinat*, as a French writer calls
it,—this Chinese system of competitive examinations, which
results in part from the high pressure of difficulties in an
over-crowded country,—has its dark and evil side ; and I
think that teachers may diminish its evils. By a little
judicious praise and encouragement, they may often dissipate
needless anxiety. They may always, in their general training, put competition on its right basis ; they may show boys
that it is not everything ; that it does not always, or often,
test the highest gifts and qualities ; that failure in it need
not be nearly so fatal to their prospects as they suppose. I
remember how Henry Martyn, in his Life, tells us how
much he was calmed and strengthened, on the eve of the
examination which left him a Senior Wrangler, by a University sermon on "Seekest thou great things for thyself ?
Seek them not, saith the Lord." We may always teach our
boys to look first and most to that competition in which no
good man can fail. We can, with Mr Ruskin, say to them,
" I want you to compete, not for the praise of what you
know, but of what you *become*, and to compete only in that

great school where Death is the Examiner and God the Judge." And our encouragement may, most of all, be needed by those who do not excel at all in the studies with which we are most directly concerned. "He took me," said Jeremy Bentham of the late Lord Lansdowne, "out of the bottomless pit of humiliation, he made me feel that I was something." I once had a pupil who did not succeed at all, or only very moderately, in the ordinary curriculum of schools. He is now a man of high political and literary distinction. I know no pupil of mine, however brilliant, who is so likely to climb to the highest things; and he always says that the self-reliance which has helped him forward could never have sprung up, but for the early and cordial recognition of power which found no play in the school routine. And, as illustrating what I have said about the encouraging recognition of merits which lie outside our ordinary school routine, I think that you will all be interested to hear a letter which I once had the honour to receive from Charles Darwin. Knowing him slightly, I sent him a lecture of mine, delivered sixteen years ago before the Royal Institution, on "Some Defects of Public Education." "I am very much obliged," he wrote, "for your kind present of your lecture. We have read it aloud with the greatest interest, and I agree to every word. If I had been a great classical scholar, I would never have been able to have judged fairly on the subject. As it is, I am one of the root-and-branch men, and would leave Classics to be learnt by those alone who have sufficient zeal, or the high taste requisite for their appreciation." Then, after very kind words to me, which I omit, he adds—"I was at school at Shrewsbury, under a great scholar, Dr Butler. I learnt absolutely nothing, except by amusing myself by reading and experimenting in chemistry. Dr Butler somehow found this out, and publicly sneered at me, before the whole school, for such gross waste of time ; I remember he called me a 'Poco Curante,' which, not understanding, I thought was a dreadful name." This letter of a great man is, I think, instructive in many ways. It illustrates our vivid memories, even to old age, of words spoken to us in early boyhood. It illustrates how undesirable it is to sneer. It shows how minds of the grandest capacity may not even be touched by an exclusively classical curriculum. It shows how much we should try to have wide appreciation of differing gifts and to be many-sided in our teaching.

II.   Hitherto I have been speaking mainly of those fundamental aims and considerations which must underlie the teacher's work. I will now venture to make some general remarks on matters intellectual and practical.

1.   I would say first, "Make a rule of regularity and faithfulness in routine duties." I would not have this rule treated with morbid and pharisaic rigidity. I would not see a teacher sink into the slave of routine. It is much more important that he should remain vigorous, fresh, in good spirits, and constantly equipped with new stores of knowledge, than that he should invariably pay tithes of mint, anise, and cummin in minor duties. Take the correction of Verses. I groan and grieve to think over the number of hours, and *days* of hours, in my life, which have been irrevocably wasted, and worse than wasted, in the execrably bad system—killing to the master and worthless to the boy —of turning boys' bad exercises into "fair copies," and transforming the crippled and hobbling lines of boys into a

wooden semblance of soundness. I hold it to be one valuable service in life that I gave one of the first, and one of the strongest, blows to the practice of teaching Latin Verses to all boys alike, which entailed no small part of this senseless and useless drudgery. I must not, however, digress into that topic, but will say that, given a human and sensible system of written exercises, they ought, as a rule, to be faithfully looked through and marked. A great man, indeed, may do without this rule. The late Bishop of Manchester, Dr Prince Lee, did not follow it. I have heard one of his illustrious pupils describe in old days, how he would sometimes have a whole drawerful of uncorrected exercises, and then, summoning up a boy, would take one of the exercises, almost at random, and correct it or criticise it in such a way as the boy never forgot. With such a man as Prince Lee such a system will work well; but, if an ordinary man does not make a rule of noticing his boys' written work, they will assuredly cease to take pains with it. A Headmaster once told me that he had never quite got over the pain he felt because *his* old Head-master never so much as looked at a particular exercise with which he had taken extraordinary pains, and which he considered to be the best he had ever written.

2. Then I will say,—Always, even for the lowest form, *prepare your work*, or at least look at it beforehand. A Scripture lesson, a History lesson, even a construing lesson of ten or twenty lines, will be better and fresher by far, if you have at least glanced it over; much more if you have considered beforehand how best you can bring it out. Perhaps you will tell me that Dr Arnold by no means always prepared his lessons. "Any hard word in the Aristophanes?"

so one of his pupils tells me he used sometimes to say before a lesson; "if so, I shall be floored." But this, perhaps, was the reason why Dr Arnold fell into little scholarship-traps, which some of his best pupils were sometimes audacious enough to lay for him. He never pretended to know what he did not know, and would always pause to look out a word in his lexicon in mid-lesson before his form. But Arnold was Arnold; and a dwarf is ill-advised when he tries to array himself in the garments of a Colossus.

3. If you prepare your lessons, you will better fulfil another requisite of the teacher, which is to *make your lessons interesting.* It is a very old principle, but a very wise one. If the draught must often be unpleasant, there is no harm in tinging the rim of the cup with honey. I do not only mean that the teacher's *manner* should be free from the preternatural dulness, which makes of a lesson a veritable imprisonment to a lively boy. A story used to be told of my dear old college tutor, E. M. Cope, how, on one occasion, without changing one muscle of his face, or one intonation of his voice, he interpolated into his lecture the remark, "What I am now telling you is, I believe, entirely new and most important. It has cost me very long and toilsome research to discover it. And, exactly at this point, I observe that not a single person in the room is paying me the smallest attention." He then continued as before. But I will undertake to say that, had his manner been less despondent and more vivacious, every one would have been listening.

> "Ridentem dicere verum
> Quid vetat? ut pueris olim dant crustula blandi
> Doctores, elementa velint ut discere prima."

But, if it is important that the teacher's manner should not
be dry and dull, it is much more so that he should enlist on
his side the intellect, the reason, the imagination, the fancy.
Is it not deplorable to think, for instance, that, in old days,
we used to struggle through the sandy wilderness of number-
less inflexions, without so much as a gleam of light being
shed on us as to what an inflexion is ! Even a young child
will go through the frightful ordeal of learning the 1200
forms of a full Greek conjugation, if he has once mastered
the conception that not one of these inflexions is arbitrary,
or accidental, and that—for instance—such a form as ἐτετί-
μηντο consists of six parts, and contains the elements of at
least five words.   I undertake to say that a few hours wisely
spent in teaching a boy the nature of words, the difference
between loose prefixes and close suffixes, and the simplest
elements of philology, would spare him endless labour and
make his labour more interesting.   Is it not deplorable to
think that we used to regard the aorist as a sort of unknown
Greek monster, with no one to tell us that our own
language, strictly speaking, and apart from auxiliaries,
possessed no tenses at all except aorists ? and that the
laws of the Greek and Latin sentence were drummed into
us without so much as a hint that the optative and subjunc-
tive exist in Latin and English as well as in Greek, and are
governed by much the same laws?   Rational teaching is
always more interesting than irrational ; and, when one
only thinks of the dreary and futile toil spent by hundreds
of English lads for years together, with the result of *not*
acquiring a single Greek verb, it is at least a duty to make
the teaching as human as we can.   On the interest of the
lessons depends very much of their effect, and very much of
real as apart from dead and mechanical discipline.   When

I was a master, if my form was restless, or if boys yawned, I always primarily blamed, not them, but myself.

4. But, if you make your lessons interesting, if you succeed in inspiring your boys with any love for knowledge, you may often greatly help them forward by the influence which will enable you, without difficulty, to induce them to do private work. A boy, by no means clever, whom I wished to get on in Greek Iambics, once did for me, in his holidays, I cannot tell how many hundred verses from the beginning of Beatson's Iambics, as the result of a request so incidental that, when he told me that he had done them, I had forgotten all about it. A boy who has since become a very able Cabinet Minister, and is the heir of an old and wealthy family, once said the whole of the Agamemnon through, choruses and all, to Dr Butler, as part of his voluntary work in the holidays. Those who have read such biographies as that of Dr Young, or Mill's account of his education in his Autobiography, or the list of books got through in a country parsonage by the late brilliant Professor Henry Smith, ought at least to be aware how much may be done—done without pressure, done thoroughly, and done delightfully—by an able boy under wise guidance. If exceptional boys are rare, so are exceptional teachers; but very much more may be accomplished, even by ordinary boys and by moderate teachers, than is commonly supposed. I feel a strong conviction that, in spite of all our vaunted nineteenth-century wisdom and enlightenment, we are still, in matters of education, in a very rudimentary stage; that we follow many mistaken aims by many cumbrous and ineffectual methods; and that, except in the one matter of kindness, we are, both in theory

and practice, far behind many teachers who lived in ages which we affect to despise,—ages when athletics were not so exclusively idolised; when ladies could write and speak in Greek and Latin, as well as several modern languages; when Erasmus read by moonlight, because he could not afford a penny to buy a torch, and the boy Milton had made such striking advance by the age of ten.

5. In the same direction would be my advice to make all the use you can of *illustration.* I employ the term in its widest sense. To illustrate a subject means to throw light upon it, and men had discovered, thousands of years ago, that the memory becomes more impressible through the eye than through the ear. If you are dealing with some historical scene or character, no way of impressing facts upon the memory is comparable to that of putting your pupils into immediate contact with the person or event, by letting him see or handle something which visibly recalls it. A coin, a medal, a bust, a picture, an inscription, a relic, actually examined and handled, will do more to awaken the interest and to impress the memory than almost anything which you can say. The coins, the photographs, the casts, which can now be obtained on such easy and favourable terms from the authorities of the British Museum, are invaluable for this purpose; and I can imagine a Public School-master, at the cost of a few pounds, getting together for his own use a sort of little museum, which would constantly add life, vividness, and interest to his lessons. A boy who has seen the Elgin marbles, and has been taught to see them intelligently, will be far better able to understand Greek. A boy who has seen a good selection of fine Roman coins, will be better able to understand the era of the

Republic and of the Emperors. A boy who has actually
handled a phylactery, and seen the difference, maintained
to this day, between an ordinary phylactery and the broader
phylacteries of the modern representatives of the Pharisees,
has the germs of considerable insight into Judaism. A boy
who has read, on the fragments of the arch which once
spanned the main street of Thessalonica, and which are
now in the British Museum, the unique word πολιτάρχας,
which St Luke, with his memorable accuracy, applies to the
magistrates of Thessalonica, may be led to trace the many
strong external arguments for the minute faithfulness of the
Evangelists.

6. It is needless to multiply instances; but I would
strongly urge illustrations of quite a different character—
illustrations from historical parallels, illustrations from
modern literature, modern poetry, modern languages. I
think that, in teaching an Epistle of St Paul, a boy will
better understand the touching messages in the last chapter
of the Epistle to the Romans, who has had read to him the
exactly analogous dying messages of "the Apostle of the
High Alps," Felix Neff. He will better feel the pathos of
St Paul's request for his books and parchments and cloak,
if his attention be called to the minute but wholly unconscious parallel, supplied by Tyndale's touching letter from
his chill and melancholy prison. The letter to Philemon
will shine in brighter colours, when it is compared with
Pliny's letter to Sabinianus. The serene cheerfulness of St
Paul, in his Roman imprisonment, will appear still more
beautiful when contrasted with the way in which exile, and
trials far less intense than St Paul's, affected the minds and
writings of Cicero, of Seneca, and even of Dante. When I

was a schoolmaster, I never used to read with my form a Greek play, without the constant endeavour to compare it with modern tragedies on the same subject, and to brighten it by all the modern parallels which I could find. I think, too, that the teacher may often be helped, by calling attention to brilliant translations and imitations of classical authors by men of genius. Few translations surpass those of Conington, in their *curiosa felicitas*. What could be a happier rendering of

"Veniam petimusque damusque vicissim,"

than—

"He who needs excuse must needs excuse"?

What could bring out the spirit of

$$\text{"}\mu\eta\delta\grave{\epsilon}\ \beta\alpha\rho\beta\acute{\alpha}\rho\text{ου}\ \phi\omega\tau\grave{o}s\ \delta\acute{\iota}\kappa\eta\nu$$
$$\chi\alpha\mu\alpha\iota\pi\epsilon\tau\grave{\epsilon}s\ \beta\acute{o}\alpha\mu\alpha\ \pi\rho\sigma\chi\acute{\alpha}\nu\eta s\ \grave{\epsilon}\mu\sigma\acute{\iota}\text{,"}$$

better than the grand paraphrase of Symmonds—

"Ope not the mouth to me, nor cry amain,
As at the footstool of a man of the East
Prone on the ground: so stoop not thou to me"?

May not Thomson's

"Where the big torrent *foams its madness off*,

suggest the force of Æschylus's—

$$\text{"}\grave{\epsilon}\nu\theta\grave{\alpha}\ \pi\sigma\tau\alpha\mu\grave{o}s\ \grave{\epsilon}\kappa\phi\upsilon\sigma\hat{q}\ \mu\acute{\epsilon}\nu\sigma s\text{"}?$$

and may not a boy be interested to find half-a-dozen English parallels to ποικιλείμων νὺξ or ποντίων κυμάτων ἀνήριθμον γέλασμα? In reading Homer, may he not, with small and most fruitful expenditure of time, be relieved for a moment from the agonies of parsing, by some spirit-stirring rendering from Chapman; or may he not learn a lesson in taste and poetic criticism, if you show him the difference between Homer and the "Anti-homeric Miltonism" of Cowper, and the chasm which exists between the artificial mannerism of Pope and the true perception of Nature, in the famous simile of the sky and stars?

7. I would say, in conclusion, *Try to be many-sided.* Bear in mind that, while our present system of classical education continues, a boy who leaves in a low form has, in literal fact, spent the greater part of his time in *not* acquiring the merest rudiments of Greek accidence and Latin construction.   He may learn much from his companions, much from contact with other minds, much from the general routine and training of the school; he may have many incidental chances of knowledge : but I must say, quite deliberately, and as the result of induction from wide experience and very many testimonies, that, *so far as mere intellectual equipment is concerned*, a non-classical boy, an ordinary boy, who leaves in the low form of a public school at the age of sixteen or seventeen, has received the worst of all possible educations.   It may be the best that is to be had for him, but, as Talleyrand said, it is "execrable."   We are told of some Scotch official, who, visiting a school and making a little speech, called it "this excellent *cemetery* of education." The other day, a lady wrote to a Head-master, asking him to "*inter*" a boy in a certain public school; and he, entering into the unconscious jest, wrote back that he would "*undertake*" it.   Many a truth has been spoken in jest or by mistake, and I fear that boys not a few have been intellectually "interred" in our various "cemeteries" of education. Things are, however, far better in this respect than they were thirty, or even twenty, or even ten years ago.   Still, I

cannot but think that a little brightness, a little variety, a little imagination, might save much of our classical teaching from being needlessly infructuous. Take Mythology. Could any lesson be more suggestive, than a proof of the extent to which Mythology is, on the one hand a disease of language, on the other a poetic and imaginative conception of natural phenomena, and yet that it reflects the deepest experiences, and gives expression to the strongest moral instincts of mankind? A dozen sentences from Bacon, or from Ruskin, about Heracles, about Ixion, about Atalanta, about the Harpies, about the Nemean lion, might give a boy lessons full of poetry, imagination, and moral wisdom which he would never forget. Horace is very commonly read in all schools. I can imagine no lessons which can be made brighter, more suggestive, more instructive, even for ordinary boys, than good lessons in the Odes of Horace; and yet remember how even a boy so exceptional as Lord Byron says,—

> "It is a curse
> To *understand*, not *feel*, thy lyric flow,
> To comprehend yet never love thy verse,
> Although no better moralist rehearse
> Our little life, or bard prescribe his art,
> Or livelier satirist the conscience pierce,
> Awakening without wounding the touched heart."

I think that every teacher would be better for trying to follow the wise old orator's advice:—"Ipse aliquid, immo multa, quotidie dicat, quae secum audita referant."

It is more than time to conclude these slight hints. Let their slightness and their feebleness be pardoned, and let me only say, that the teacher who has been so blessed as to begin his high work with pure and lofty aims, and to carry

it on with intelligent and fruitful methods, has not lived in
vain.   Some, at least, of his pupils will love him, and
honour him, and be grateful to him.   Some whom he will
never see again, will yet say of him,—

> "Still may he find, as slopes life's downward tide,
> Each wish, each joy our thoughtlessness denied,
> Each passing hour a happier influence shed,
> And age steal softly on his honoured head."

Yes, it may be that some tears will be shed by those who
stand beside his grave.

Gentlemen, my work as a schoolmaster is over; but you,
too, in your turn, are going forth to your work and to your
labour until the evening.   When Lord Dalhousie was resign-
ing to Lord Canning the government of 196,000,000 people,
and was standing on the steps of Government House at
Calcutta to receive his successor, Sir John Lawrence asked
him what were his feelings at that moment.   "He had been
standing back, with a wearied look; but, immediately I put
the question," said Sir John Lawrence, "he drew himself up,
and, with great fire, replied, 'I wish that I were Canning,
and Canning I, and then wouldn't I govern India!'   Then,
of a sudden, the fire died away, and he said, 'No, I don't!
I would not wish my greatest enemy, much less my friend
Canning, to be the poor, miserable, broken-down, dying
man that I am.'"   Gentlemen, I, too, feel inclined to say,—
I wish that I were now in your place, and then wouldn't
I teach!   But, no,—"Morituri vos salutamus."   Thirteen
years afterwards, the very same question, "What are your
feelings at this moment?" was put to Lord Lawrence—Iron
John—when he, too, stood on the same spot, and under

the same circumstances, awaiting his successor, Lord Mayo; and he answered, "It was a proud moment to me when I walked up the steps of this house. But it will be a happier moment when I walk down the steps with the feeling that I have tried to do my duty[1]." What better wish can an old teacher offer to you, than that each of you, when you step for the last time from the Master's chair, may feel that you, too, have "tried to do your duty"?

[1] For this deeply instructive anecdote see the admirable life of Lord Lawrence by my friend Mr Bosworth Smith.

FORM MANAGEMENT.

By R. B. POOLE, B.D.

HEAD MASTER OF BEDFORD MODERN SCHOOL.

FORM MANAGEMENT.

I MUST at the commencement of my Lecture attempt
to some extent to disarm criticism by apologizing for the
commonplace and practical nature of the remarks I am
about to offer. I have never, I regret to say, given much
attention to the Theory of Education, partly because it
was not so much thought of and discussed at the time when I
first became a schoolmaster as it is now, and partly because
I have never known what it was to have much leisure time :
and so, as has been no doubt the case with many others,

> "The art and practic part of life
> Must be the mistress to this theoric."

I venture, however, to take courage from the fact that it
was suggested that the subject should be a practical one,
and also from seeing that many of those who have lectured
before me have contented themselves with adopting a
similar line, and that most, if not all of them, have been
schoolmasters themselves. And I must also apologize if I
should be found here and there to tread somewhat too
closely in the steps of my predecessors. If I have done so
it is quite unwittingly, for I only received a copy of the
Lectures, which have been previously given under the
auspices of this Syndicate, yesterday morning, and so have

not had an opportunity of finding out the exact lines which they follow. If I have erred in this respect it must be attributed to the fact that there are many things which naturally come into the minds of practical schoolmasters when speaking on subjects connected with Education.

And perhaps I may be here allowed to observe that it seems to me a most excellent thought on the part of the promoters of these lectures to give men who are likely to adopt teaching as a profession an opportunity of gathering something from the experience of those who have gone before them. It would be hard if, after a score of years of work with boys, one had not something to say about their management, and it would be curious if Teaching were the only profession into which a man could enter with success without any previous training, especially considering the various and delicate subjects with which masters have to deal. And yet I am afraid that it *is* a profession which many enter because they do not see their way to anything else, and because as a rule a degree is an immediate passport to it.

I propose to speak to you to-day principally on the subject of Form Management, although it may be necessary from time to time to allude also to the management of Sets. The distinction between the two is probably familiar to all of you, but, in case it should not be so, I will briefly explain it. There is in all schools with which I am acquainted some staple subject, or subjects, upon which the reputation of the school principally depends and which determines the position of each boy. Where there are separate departments, or sides, as at Marlborough, Cheltenham, Clifton and other places, there are practically so many separate schools, as far as classification is concerned. The Classical Side will be arranged according to the boys' classical attainments; the Modern according to their Historical, Mathematical, and Scientific abilities, or their proficiency in modern languages ; the Military generally will depend mainly upon its mathematics. As many subjects as possible will be taught according to this classification, but there will always be some, of less weight on the particular side in question, for the teaching of which a different classification will be necessary. These are generally spoken of as "Sets", while the arrangement upon which a boy's status in the school and his promotion depends is called his "Form". It is with the management of the latter that I am principally concerned on the present occasion.

The duties of a Form Master are far more varied and in some ways more responsible than those of a Set Master, and his influence is more decidedly felt. He naturally sees more of each individual boy under him, has more opportunity of studying his character, and of judging of his capabilities and tastes as a whole. He ought, if he understands his work well, to be able to suggest the best ways of managing a boy, and of developing his character and powers. A Set master only sees each class for some three or four hours in the week, and most likely in only one subject, which may be that subject in which a given boy is weakest or which he dislikes, or on the contrary that in which he specially excels. Thus it is, I think, desirable that a Set master should consult the Form master before inflicting any severe punishment on a boy, in order that he may be informed whether the conduct with which he has to find fault, or the idleness which he thinks he sees in him, pervades all his work, or whether it is exceptional. I have known instances in which a Set master has entirely misunderstood a boy, and has perhaps by some punishment wholly demoralized one whose general career is far above the average. This is, I need scarcely say, a result very much to be deplored, and one which might have been altogether obviated by a consultation with the master who knew him best. In fact the Form master ought to look upon himself, and be looked upon by others, as a sort of family doctor, who thoroughly understands the constitution of his patients, and feels a certain amount of jealousy if his general treatment is interfered with by some one who is, as it were, only called in occasionally.

I am disposed to think that it is a good thing as far as possible to confine the teaching of a Form to one man. This can easily be done in lower Forms, but cannot well be managed higher up in a school, as it would be nearly impossible to find a man of such varied attainments as to be able to take a high Form in everything, or nearly everything. And it is more important that it should be so with smaller than with bigger boys. For the former, as a rule, take less interest in their work, and cannot be so easily appealed to as the latter; and they have less appreciation of the value of the knowledge they are gaining, or of the teaching they are receiving. I have known instances of men of high attainments who seemed quite incapable of keeping little boys in order, but who were listened to with the greatest respect and interest by those who were capable of understanding the value of the scholarship and knowledge which was quite wasted on the others.

One more remark I must make about Set masters, before turning entirely to the question of Form Management, and that is that their difficulties are very great, and that a man who is successful in this post would almost invariably and *a fortiori* make an excellent Form master. For a large number of boys are constantly passing through a Set master's hands over whom it is not easy to get much personal influence. He goes from one Set to another, hour after hour, and thus has much less chance of impressing his individuality upon·them. In my opinion his best plan, if he wishes to be a success, is to see as much as he possibly can of the boys out of school, to join in games, or some school institutions such as the Debating or Scientific Societies, or the Rifle Corps, and as occasion serves to invite boys to his house or rooms, and to get to know something of them. In all probability, if he has a specialité, as most Set masters are likely to have, he will thus acquire the respect and friendship of a sufficient number of boys to leaven the classes he has to teach, and by degrees it will become known throughout the school that he is deserving of that affection which boys very seldom withhold from those who take a real interest in them.

I now revert to a Form master's work, or Form Management, which is the subject of this Lecture. And I propose to touch somewhat briefly, but perhaps a little discursively, upon five aspects of the life of a Form : (1) its Tone, (2) its Work, (3) Marking, (4) Discipline, and (5) Games.

1. I need scarcely say that the 'tone' of a Form is of the greatest possible importance both to the moral and intellectual condition of the boys who compose it ; and it must be borne in mind that the tone of the school depends upon the condition of the different Forms which make up

the whole. When this is bad in any given Form it is principally the fault of the master, for it is not likely that there should be a large proportion of intractable or vicious boys out of some 25 or 30, although there will most likely always be a few. The great point is to get the majority into the right way of thinking about things, and then the few black sheep will not be able to exercise much influence. The first step in the right direction is for the master to gain the confidence of the boys, and to make them feel that he is working for them and with them, and has no object except their advantage and benefit. I have known some masters who enter their class-rooms with the evident feeling that they will find the boys antagonistic to them, and seem to be on the look out for something with which they may find fault. Such as these appear to fear that, if they unbend at all, it will be to the loss of their own dignity, and thus they repel confidence and keep their pupils at arms' length. This is generally the result of want of confidence and consciousness of power; sometimes of nervous sensitiveness; sometimes of merely an unsympathetic nature. In any of these cases a man is not likely to make a good schoolmaster from the highest point of view, though he may possibly be able to teach well. It is quite true that a master should always be able to resume his dignity, even if he has seemed to forget it for a while, but his general attitude should be that of the friend deeply interested in the welfare of those about him, and forgetful of himself in his thought for them. It is not easy to get to this position *in the class-room only*. By far the best way, as has been hinted before, is for a master to ask boys occasionally to his rooms, to drop his official position as far as would be consistent, to draw out the boys' inner selves, to learn something of their homes and belongings, of their ideas on general matters, of their future career, and of what they think about school affairs. If he is unable to do this, as may sometimes be the case, he should take opportunities of walking and talking with them out of school, and in this way show the interest he takes in them. It is nearly impossible for this sort of treatment to be thrown away. Boys are naturally affectionate and sympathetic, and they will keenly feel a reproof from one who, they know, likes them and cares for them; they will hesitate to deceive him in any way, and will certainly cease to look upon him as their natural enemy, even if they have been inclined to do so before.

This leads me to one way in which a Form master may largely assist the general condition of a school. He should strongly impress his boys with the feeling that he is as much a part of the form as they are, and that therefore, if they disgrace themselves in any way, they bring disgrace upon the Form and upon him. If this idea be firmly established it will be of the greatest possible assistance to Set masters, who, as has been noticed, are somewhat handicapped, in keeping good discipline, as compared with Form masters. And this feeling will be carried even beyond the bounds of the school itself, and will affect the general demeanour of the boys under almost all circumstances. I may illustrate this by saying that I have known cases of parallel Forms being remarkable for their totally different behaviour with the same Set master. In this case the fault must have lain with the Form master, for the boys were of about the same age, the same attainments, and not sorted into forms from their being troublesome or the reverse.

Another point of extreme importance is to have a very high standard with reference to fair dealing on the part of the boys. My own experience goes to show that there are few things more difficult to insist on than this, and there are many reasons why it should be so. In the first place it is very difficult to make boys see that *small* dishonesties are so reprehensible as they are. Most will understand that copying in examination, or looking at books during lessons, or copying an exercise from another are wrong, but they do not regard the use of translations, or asking questions from others so as to save themselves trouble, or doing an exercise with a boy much cleverer than themselves, or writing the English of words down in their books, in the same light. This is due I think to two causes—one, that there is a considerable laxity in public opinion on these points—the other, that a boy does not see much harm in doing something not strictly straightforward, if it is merely done *to save himself,* though he would not do it if he thought he would really injure the chances of another boy. There are a large number of people of what I may call the "old school," who often tell with considerable gusto how they successfully hoodwinked their masters in their schoolboy days : and I am afraid too that in many of the public examinations of the present day there is considerable laxness in the view taken of what is fair and honourable.

It is to me very strange to hear, as one sometimes does, people drawing a strong distinction between the amount of fairness which ought to be observed in a *pass* as compared with a *competitive* examination, as though a man was perfectly justified in carrying about with him a certificate for proficiency which he does not deserve, and which enables him to sail under false colours, though he would not be justified in obtaining a place in competition with others by the same means. No doubt in some senses, viewed as to its consequences, the latter is the worse case, but both are equally dishonest. Hence it seems to me that Form masters will do a great work if they check even the smallest kinds of unfairness in early life, and by that means establish a habit which will hold its own through a man's whole subsequent career. I have always found that, with older boys, the best way is to explain to them that any work shown up which is not absolutely their own is a species of theft, inasmuch as they are claiming that as theirs which in reality belongs to someone else, and that moreover a place gained in this way over another may affect his future life to an extent which they would scarcely realize, and of which it never entered their heads to dream. That it does so sometimes there can be no doubt. It may happen that a boy just fails to get removed to a higher form, and in consequence his career at school is cut short; or he may not be allowed to go to the University, as he was intended to do. Now if this place has been taken from him by a boy who has been guilty of unfair dealing even of the most trivial character, he has inflicted just as much injury upon him as he would have done had he taken a place above him by the same means in a competitive examination. Again, I need scarcely say that a master should never have any favourites, at any rate, not *visible* favourites. It may not be possible to care for all boys alike, but it is certainly possible not to show any individual partiality. The effect of doing so is to shake the general confidence in the master's fairness, to dishearten some boys, and to make others lazy, from a feeling that their faults, or want of preparation, will be viewed in an indulgent light.

Great care should be taken to distinguish between moral faults and mere silliness. Sometimes masters seem to view these all alike, and to treat them in the same way. The former should be treated with the utmost seriousness, and generally with severity; while a stop may generally be put to the latter by "chaff." But this must be successful "chaff," and must be of such a character as to make the rest of the form laugh *at*, not *with* the offender, otherwise I need not say it will entirely fail in its object. Idleness or ignorance may be treated in the same way, but with more circumspection, as sometimes apparent neglect may be only due to want of ability. This "chaff" should always be good-natured, not too sarcastic and cutting, for while desiring to correct the fault a master should always be careful not to hurt the feelings. I have known boys imbibe a perfect hatred for a master on account of the bitter things which have been said to them, and thus his whole object has been defeated.

We will now proceed to consider the example which should be set by the master himself in his own work and conduct so as to raise and improve the tone of his Form in some other respects. In the first place, then, he should give his whole attention to the work in which he is engaged, and never allow himself to do anything during school time either in the way of private work or reading. Of course sometimes it may be necessary to attend to some urgent matter, but I am speaking of the general rule and not of its exceptions. I have known masters who were in the habit of reading newspapers, or books unconnected with their work, or writing letters in school. These things have a bad effect in at least two ways, for they obviously distract the master's attention, and so prevent his noticing what may be going on in his Form, and they also shake the confidence of the boys in their teacher when they see that his thoughts are taken up with other things. He can scarcely expect that

they will give their whole energy to what they are doing if
he does not do so himself, and hence the Form will become
slack and indifferent. Such a state of things too fosters the
practice of unfair dealing, for it renders the chance of de-
tection much more doubtful.

The last special point I will mention in reference to the
general tone of a Form is one which may seem trivial in
character, but of which the importance may, I think, be
underrated. And that is insisting upon the external appearance of the boys being suitable to their school and
to their position as school-boys. And in this matter it
is necessary to guard against both excess and defect. On
the one hand boys should be taught to be neat and clean in
their dress and appearance, so that proper self-respect for
their outward man may be duly inculcated, and on the
other great care should be taken to repress any love of
flashy dressing, and the wearing of flashy jewellery. One
of the great fears of the present day is that boys should
think themselves men before their time, not in manly
sports, or, in a word, in true manliness, but rather in
that precociousness which, in its inexperience, apes the
worst qualities of grown-up people, and mistakes a swagger-
ing demeanour for moral courage, and a proper feeling of
independence and self-reliance. To show how a master may
exercise influence in this respect, I may mention how
deeply a little incident of this sort was in my early days
at Rugby impressed upon my mind. I remember that once
when the newly-elected Archbishop of Canterbury was
giving out a copy of verses, he happened to see a boy with
a ring on his finger, which he was looking at in an admiring
manner. He was promptly told to take it off, and never
appear at school with it again. I recollect well thinking

how foolish the boy looked when he had to take off his treasure, and deposit it in his pocket, and I do not think the little lesson was altogether lost on all of us. At any rate it produced so vivid an impression on my mind that I have never forgotten it from that day to this.

To sum up our considerations then on this head, we may observe what a great power a Form master may be in moulding the character of the boys under him, by creating a manly, straightforward and honourable tone among them, and how much he may contribute to the general tone and feeling of the school in which he is a master. No doubt a high character and great conscientiousness is required to carry all these things out, but the more we reflect upon the great responsibilities of our position as trainers of the young the more shall we feel the great necessity for these qualities, as well as others, if we wish to do our duty thoroughly, and to raise the character of all branches of our profession. If these things had been more thought of in times gone by, there would never have been that slight stigma attached in the public mind to our avocation, which arose in generations long since gone in consequence, partly at any rate, of a want of that high standard which is I believe now generally proposed to themselves by those who join our ranks.

2. I now pass on to the second head of my subject, that is to say, Form work. And here I wish to be especially practical, but trust that in being so I shall not seem to descend too much into detail. Most of those points which I am about to mention have to be impressed upon young masters, and though in consequence of the advantages which the labours of this Syndicate offer, they may be less

needed than formerly, yet still they will perhaps bear to be briefly laid before those who think of making teaching their profession.

And first I cannot impress too strongly upon you that all lessons should be *prepared* by the master before he goes into school. The amount of preparation may be, great or little, according to the subject taught and the Form taken, but I do not think that there is any exception to this rule. Those lessons which partake of the nature of lectures, or which actually *are* lectures, of course need the greatest care, and often a good deal of reading. History, Geography and Literature perhaps need the most : Science comes next, and then Languages and Mathematics—but all need some. Even with a low Classical Form it is well to look over a lesson of Latin or Greek, if it be only in order to see what special constructions therein contained it will be best to impress upon the boys' minds, and how the best use may be made of the hour or period allotted to the lesson. In History especially, a master will meet with ample reward in the interest he will create, if he is able to illustrate copiously and readily the period he is reading from other sources than the text-books which the boys are using. It may be argued that most well educated men who are competent to teach the subject will naturally be able and ready to do this from their own stock of knowledge. No doubt they may be so, but I am quite sure that they will greatly gain in clearness and lucidity of argument if they have made up their minds what they are going to say, and have arranged it methodically in their own minds. In giving lessons of this kind, as is usual in most things, the extremes should be avoided, and the mean observed. A master should not be too professorial, that is to say he should not do all the talking himself, and omit to question the boys in the subject they are doing, nor on the other hand should he merely make sure that they have prepared the lesson, and do no more than see that they have mastered what their text-book teaches them. In the former case, boys soon get to know that they do not gain anything as far as marks are concerned, by preparing their work, in the latter they have no new lights thrown upon the subject and so lose interest, and gain no more by saying the lesson to the master than they may have already done by preparing it carefully themselves. Yet we must remember that this careful preparation on the part of the boys must always be exacted. If it is not, the subject will not be fully grasped at the time, nor will it remain firmly fixed in the memory.

The next point I will touch upon is that of Exercises or written work, whether done in school or out. These should always be marked, and the mistakes underlined by the *master himself*, and that for many reasons. By some people the plan is adopted of allowing the boys to exchange exercises one with another, especially when they are of such a kind that the right answer cannot vary, and then allowing each boy to correct his neighbour's paper, while the master gives the right answer. It seems to me that this plan throws great temptations into the way of the boys of committing some sort of unfairness. A small boy may be easily compelled by a bigger one to pass over some of his mistakes, or another may do the same thing for the sake of his friend. Besides this an inexperienced eye often fails to detect mistakes, and thus the marking may be incorrect. I am aware that there is some advantage in the plan, especially that it causes boys to look carefully to see what is right and what is wrong, and that thus they may learn a good deal. It may also be urged that if a master collects the exercises or papers afterwards, and looks over a certain number so that the boys may think it likely that any unfairness will be detected, they will in all probability be careful to mark the mistakes as correctly as they can. But even then when a paper has been a good deal marked and corrected it is often difficult to see what the original was. Hence on the whole this system should be discouraged. Generally speaking, where it is carried on to any great extent, it arises, I think, from the desire of the master to save himself trouble. There is another thing to be said too in favour of all exercises being looked over by the master, and that is that in doing so he gets to be well acquainted with the mistakes peculiar to certain boys, and also with those prevalent in his Form, and hence he will be able to correct individual errors better and to supply the deficiencies in the knowledge of given boys, and also to perceive where his own teaching has been at fault, and to discover those points which it will be well for him to emphasize.

While on this subject it will· be well to notice that written work should be looked over as soon as possible after it has been done, and returned to the boys as soon as possible; otherwise less interest will be taken in it and the line of reasoning (if any) which produced a mistake will have faded from the mind. I recollect sometimes at school not getting my copies back till as much as a month after they had been done, and having forgotten nearly all about them. Besides a mistake once made is likely to be repeated until it has been corrected, so that the sooner it is explained the better.

As to the amount of written work which is given in

4—2

a Form there will be a considerable variety of opinion, and there probably ought to be a good deal of difference between different Forms according to their position in the school. I am not in favour of giving much of it to younger boys. No doubt it fosters accuracy and discourages guessing by tying them down to one distinct statement. But this may be dearly purchased by the loss of interest and keenness which is promoted by vivâ voce teaching, and also by the fact that a great deal is learnt from the answers of others, which is not the case when the answers to questions are all written down. Of course I am not now speaking of examinations, the purpose of which is not so much to impart fresh knowledge, as to find out what has been already acquired. With older boys the case is somewhat different, as it is more necessary for them to be getting into the way of answering questions on paper, with a view to competitive and other examinations, and also because they do not need quite so much the stimulus which vivâ voce work gives, or at any rate ought not to need it. Probably the best plan, when there is time to carry it out, will be to spend some portion of the time allotted to the lesson in vivâ voce and the rest in giving a few questions to be answered on paper. This could not be applied to all lessons, and will hold good most in History, Literature and kindred subjects.

I will notice only one other point under this head, and that is that in lower Forms masters should be constantly going about among the boys while they are writing, to see how they are getting on and what they are doing. In teaching Arithmetic, and the elements of Latin Prose, I think this plan is particularly useful. In the former especially if a master goes from boy to boy, correcting his mistakes, and marking as he goes, he will not only prevent his getting stranded over some difficulty, but he will stimulate him to exertion and prevent playing or idleness. In the latter too he will prevent the recurrence of the same mistake, which may otherwise have vitiated the whole exercise for want of explanation at the outset. It will save him time also in the end, for he can mark each sum or sentence as it is done. All this requires a good deal of exertion, and makes a lesson no easy task. Indeed I do not say that it can always be expected, but I am merely endeavouring to point out what seem to me to be the most efficient methods.

3. These remarks naturally lead me to my third head— Marking. This is a subject which I am aware has already been most ably handled in this place, and I shall therefore only speak of it in a general way, in order to the completeness of my general subject of "Form Management."

There are those who are of opinion that it would be better if teaching could be carried on without any marks, considering that the eagerness to get them, which is so often found in boys, fosters a mercenary spirit, and tempts them to dishonest work. They would argue that knowledge ought to be sought for its own sake, and that if a master can infuse a proper amount of stimulus into his teaching boys may be made to work just as well without marks as with them. I do not say that there is not a good deal in this idea, but I am sure that it is too Utopian. Independently of the difficulty which would arise in promoting from one Form or Set to another, and the opening which would thus be given to accusations of favouritism on the part of masters, I feel quite sure that the average schoolboy has not arrived at that mental condition in which he would do his work to the best

of his ability for its own sake.   In fact I have no doubt that
the attempt to carry out this theory would be attended with
a complete collapse of the work of a school, if not immediately, at any rate in a short time.   Granting then that
marking is necessary, I would observe in the first place that
in every school there should be a careful and even elaborate
system according to which marks are to be awarded.   The
maxima for each subject should be fixed according to its
importance, or what practically comes to the same thing,
according to the number of hours given to it.   I am myself
strongly in favour of having the marks of the highest boy in
each Form raised to the maximum each week in each subject,
in order that the due proportion between each branch of
study may be maintained.   For it may and often does
happen, that out of a given number of marks one master is
inclined to give more than another for a particular standard
of excellence, and that thus the amount gained out of a
given maximum in one subject, may be permanently in
excess of that gained out of the same maximum in another
subject.   Hence the principle on which the marks have been
originally assigned will be practically abrogated, and of two
subjects which are considered of equal value one will always
count more than the other.   When this plan is adopted, the
marks of the whole Form or Set should be raised in the same
proportion as those of the highest boy in the subject.   There
is a certain amount of labour involved in this plan, but is
amply compensated for by the accuracy and fairness of the
result obtained.   I first became familiar with this plan at
Clifton College, and have since always carried it out, and
have found the results perfectly satisfactory.

In the second place, it is impossible that a master can be
too careful in apportioning his marks.   If he is not they fail

'of their object, for let a boy once fancy that he is not treated fairly in this respect, and he will lose that stimulus to exertion which, as I pointed out before, is the great advantage of having marks at all. Besides, the master himself will get a character for unfairness, whether deserved or not, and he will thus lose a great deal of influence over his Form.

It is desirable, I think, that boys should be allowed to see their marks if they wish to do so, for two reasons; the first, that they may have perfect confidence in the impartiality of their master; and the second, that they may have an opportunity of discovering in what points they have failed, in order that they may give special attention to them for the future.

There are, speaking roughly, two ways in which a Form may be marked, one by taking places and counting down, the other by giving a certain mark for each answer. This is of course independent of marks given for written work. Of these two systems the former is I think the better for lower Forms, the latter for higher. Place-taking certainly serves to keep the boys alive and on the alert, it makes them pay attention to what others are saying, and seems a more tangible reward at the time. Besides this, if properly carried out, it tends to make a boy work at subjects which he does not like as well as at those which he does like. This remark is based upon the supposition that each boy takes at the next lesson, whatever it may be, the place he has occupied at that which has immediately preceded it. For instance, let us suppose that a Latin lesson has been said, and that a certain boy has got to the top of the Form who dislikes History, which is the first lesson the next day. Although the subject is not congenial to him he will make a point of working hard at the History in order that he may keep his place, a thing which otherwise he would most probably not have done. Thus there is a very considerable amount of stimulus about this plan, for there are very few boys who are not pretty good in some one subject, in which they may hope to get up, and the very fact of their having once taken a good place re-acts upon the whole of their work, and makes them try as hard as they can to keep in other lessons the position they have gained in their favourite subject. But if the plan of placing boys at each lesson according to their last place in *the same subject* be adopted, not only will the general stimulus to their work be withdrawn, but finding, as they will, that the subjects in which they are weak drag them down to a low place in their week's total, they will be inclined to give up the whole thing as hopeless, and to cease to work even at those lessons for which they have a natural liking and in which otherwise they might excel. It has sometimes been advanced against "place-taking" that it is a rough and ready method, and often unfair. A ready method it certainly is, but as far as my experience goes, neither rough or unfair. If the promotions into a higher Form were settled by one day's work only under this system, I will grant that it might easily happen that the best boy might not come out first, but in the long run I feel sure that it is quite as fair, if not more so, than any other plan, and that it has in addition all the advantages which I have endeavoured to lay before you. Of course like any other system it requires to be carefully administered, and may be easily spoiled. Questions, for instance, should be asked in rotation. If a place is taken the next should be put to the boy next below him who has just gone up—in order that the same boy may not lose more than one place at a time, unless indeed in an exceptional case, when there is reason to think that there has been culpable neglect in the preparation of the lesson.

I cannot help fearing that I shall weary you with these apparently trivial matters, but the fact is that our work consists largely of these details, and it often happens that a man is successful or not as a schoolmaster according to the amount of attention he bestows upon them.

There is not much to be said upon the general aspect of the other system—that of marking according to the answers given. It is undoubtedly the best plan in higher Forms. The stimulus of place-taking ought not to be necessary when boys get towards the top of a school, as they will have other reasons for exerting themselves, in the shape of a real desire for knowledge, and the consciousness of impending examinations. Besides, in higher Forms it will be necessary for boys to be constantly taking notes, and therefore it would be extremely inconvenient for them to be repeatedly changing places, even if it were desirable on other grounds.

4. I now come to the fourth head which I laid down for consideration—Form Discipline. It is scarcely necessary for me to say that this is of the greatest importance, in fact, the want of it will paralyse the whole of a Master's work, and will make the efforts of the best teacher and the most able scholar comparatively useless. Those boys who are really anxious to learn may make fair progress, but not nearly so much as they would if the discipline were good, but the great bulk of the Form will learn next to nothing. It is well nigh impossible to lay down rules for the preservation of discipline. Everything depends upon the character, the strong will and determination of the Master. There are some men whom boys would never think of

"humbugging" as they call it—others with whom they would "try it on" at once. On these points boys are excellent judges. The great thing is to *begin* well, to show, to put it plainly, that you don't intend "to stand any nonsense," and when that fact has once been established, to win them over by kindness, and by taking interest in their work and games alike. A master who is successful in this respect will feel, and let the boys feel, that he is, and intends to remain, master of the situation, but that he is actuated in all he does by the sincere desire for the highest welfare of those committed to his charge. This, coupled with the knowledge that there is a reserve force behind, will make him both popular and respected. Very great difference has to be made between the treatment of older and younger boys. It is simply impossible to manage them in the same way. In the case of the former their reason and self-respect, and to some extent their rising feelings of independence and self-reliance, must be appealed to. There are few greater mistakes a schoolmaster can make than to bully or browbeat a boy who is approaching manhood. If he is treated in this way he will probably become defiant, and when matters have reached this pitch the situation is one of extreme tension and danger, and the only alternative may be a boy's removal from the school. It must be remembered that confidence cannot be reposed in a boy without encouraging him to express himself in a more unreserved manner, and this sometimes bears the appearance of "uppishness," if I may be allowed to use the word, to those who do not understand the character with which they are dealing, and who fail to make allowance for the "amour propre" which is beginning to spring up in a boy's mind. I know of few things which call for a greater display of tact

than the management of a class or set of boys at the top of
a large school. Sympathy with them seems to me the first
requirement, coupled with a high moral tone and firmness
when necessary. It must be remembered too that they are
at the "awkward age" between boyhood and manhood, and
that therefore allowance must be made for the follies which
belong to the earlier period, and are not yet altogether put
away, while they are gradually being trained for the responsibilities which come with maturer years.

With younger boys the case is not nearly so complex.
Although no doubt with them too the qualities mentioned
above will be wanted, viz. a high moral tone, sympathy and
firmness—yet it will not be necessary to appeal so much to
their reason, but rather to insist on unquestioning obedience.
Discipline with them should be of rather a stricter type,
though not less kindly and considerate.

With this question of Discipline there is necessarily
connected the means which should be used to enforce it,
and to get the proper amount of work out of the boys.
With those in the upper part of the school, as I have
previously hinted, a great deal may be done by making idle
or troublesome boys ridiculous in the eyes of their school-
fellows, by what for want of a better term I must call good-
humoured "chaff." I was for some time in the Form and
house of one of the greatest schoolmasters of the present
day (the Dean of Westminster) and, except for being late
in the morning, for which a fixed amount of English Repeti-
tion had to be learnt, I do not recollect his ever setting an
imposition; and I am quite sure that there was no master
at Rugby in his day for whom boys worked harder, from
whom they learnt more, or whose Form was in a better
condition. Those who have been under him will well

remember the fear they had of making careless blunders, or
coming up with an unprepared lesson; knowing how extremely foolish they would be made to look, and how
ashamed of themselves they would probably feel. No
doubt behind all this there must be a reserve of punishment
if necessary, but it will not often be required.

In the case of lower Forms, where this kind of treatment
will not be so effective, punishments of various sorts must
be employed. These should, as far as possible, be in ac-
cordance with the nature of the offence. For neglect of
work I feel sure that the best plan is to keep a boy in till
he has done it properly. In the first place there are few
things which he dislikes more than finding himself still in
school while all the others are out and enjoying themselves
in various ways. Moreover it makes him see the folly of
neglecting to prepare his work at the proper time, if he finds
that he has to do it all the same in the end. Thirdly, it is
good for the general standard of the work of the Form, as it
keeps all the members of it more or less up to the mark;
and lastly, it shows that the master is in earnest, and means
to have the work done, and that he is willing to sacrifice
himself, provided that by so doing he can really benefit the
boys. Merely setting an imposition does not have this
effect, as it can be done whenever it suits the boy's con-
venience, and involves no self-sacrifice on the part of the
master. It is easy enough to set so many lines to be
written, and hence is often done merely to save trouble,
and without regard to the real welfare of the offender.
I may as well mention here what may seem a matter of
course, but which for all that is not always done, viz. that if
boys are to be kept in the master should be careful not to
forget to come; and that if he sets an imposition, he should

always remember to exact it. I should not have drawn your attention to this had I not known of instances in which boys were in the habit of "forgetting" to come to detention and "forgetting" to do their impositions, on the off chance that they would never hear anything more about it. This is obviously bad for the boys, and detrimental to the influence of the master. For constant playfulness or inattention or other trivial faults, either detention for a short time, or some imposition, which when done will have been of some use, will be the best. If lines are set (and this should be as seldom as possible) the amount should not be excessive, but good writing ought always to be insisted upon. To tie half a dozen pens together, and with that weapon to write "Irim de caelo misit Saturnia Juno" (which I believe has fewer letters in it than any other whole line in Vergil) five or six hundred times, is not likely to be of much good to anybody, and is very likely to spoil, or help to spoil, a boy's handwriting.

There is another form of punishment sometimes adopted which is, I think, very objectionable, and that is taking away marks for any other offence than neglect of work. It is no doubt a very easy method, but it is not punishment in kind. It is not desirable that a clever boy should be kept back because he is talkative or playful, and this taking away of marks may prevent his promotion, or it may make him idle as well as otherwise troublesome, if he loses his reward for what he really does well. This should be specially borne in mind in place-taking Forms, where it is most common. For it is a very easy and ready method of punishment to tell a boy to go down three or four places, or even to send him to the bottom; and though the effect may now and then be good, I believe that on the whole it is demoralizing and therefore dangerous.

It remains to say a few words upon corporal punishment in connection with discipline. We hear a good deal said from time to time in favour of doing away with this altogether, and there are some schools, and one very large and important one, University College School, where the discipline is effectually maintained without it. But I cannot say that personally I am in favour of its abolition. It has the merit of being short, sharp, and decisive: it often brings a boy to his senses who would sulk under a long series of impositions or detentions, and to whose reason or affections it may be comparatively useless to appeal: it does not deprive a boy of that exercise which is so needful to his bodily health, and which is one of the great disadvantages of prolonged indoor work, and moreover there are some cases, such as bullying, in which its infliction is extremely appropriate. It ought, however, in my opinion, to be subject to careful restrictions, and to be made use of as seldom as possible. Where Form masters are allowed the use of the cane, it should be kept as much as possible in the background, and only brought out when it is going to be used, and that in a solemn and judicial manner. Few things are more objectionable than to see a master giving a lesson with a cane in his hand, or beside him, of which he makes use on every convenient occasion. There can be no doubt that the weaker a master is, and the smaller the amount of the influence which he has over his boys, the more frequent will be his use of the cane. In my opinion the amount of punishment of this kind which may be inflicted by an assistant master ought to be limited, as if the matter is sufficiently serious to need a very severe caning, it is also sufficiently serious to be brought before the notice of the Head-master. In cases of bullying, as I said just now, corporal punishment seems to

me most appropriate. Not only does he who wantonly
inflicts pain on his schoolfellow deserve to suffer it himself,
but as a bully is generally a coward, he particularly dreads
it. For serious moral offences also, such as lying, cheating,
or cases of petty theft, it is, I think, necessary to have punishments of this kind to which resort may be had. If it is
not so, nothing remains except expulsion, and a boy may
thus have his prospects spoiled for life, who might have been
reclaimed without recourse having been had to such an
extreme measure. I cannot help thinking that there is a
great deal of unnecessary sentimentalism involved in the
matter. All I can say is that, after twenty years' experience,
I am strongly in favour of the retention of corporal punishment, although the more I see of its effects and dangers, the
more necessary I feel it to be that careful restrictions should
be put upon it to guard against its abuse, and that if possible
it should be altogether avoided in the case of older boys.
There is one word I should like to add by way of warning to
those who intend to follow the profession of teachers, and
who will be very likely to have to begin with a Form of
young boys, and that is to guard against losing their temper,
and striking boys on the ears, or head, or indeed anywhere,
in a momentary impulse of anger. Real physical harm may
be done in this way, the indignation of parents may be most
disagreeably and yet justly aroused, and at any rate no good
whatever is likely to come of it.

5. I now pass on to my last head, and will offer a few
remarks on the subject of games in connection with Form
Management. On this point I will not detain you long,
but it is perhaps desirable to mention it, as some of those
who undertake school work seem to think that their re-

sponsibility altogether ends when the school hours are over, although I am glad to say that the number of such people is constantly diminishing.

A master then should take an interest in the games of the school, and in those of his own Form in particular. He should urge boys to play, and if he can do so, he should play himself. I will content myself with two reasons : the first, which has been alluded to before, that he will increase enormously his influence over the boys with whom he has to do; the second, that playing thoroughly at school games is a most desirable—I had well nigh said necessary—thing for a boy's physique and health, and perhaps the very best way of keeping him from falling into vicious habits, which some day may prove his ruin both in body and soul. The whole subject with which this is connected has been most ably treated by the present Head master of Clifton College, in a paper read by him some short time ago before the Education Society, and since published in the form of a pamphlet. I can most strongly recommend it to the careful perusal of those who are thinking of entering the scholastic profession.

The time has now come for this lecture to close, and I must once more apologize to my audience for the extremely commonplace nature of my remarks, and for what may seem the trivial details into which I have entered. All that I have said will be quite familiar to those who have them- selves had any experience in school work, but I have acted on the supposition—whether right or wrong—that the object of these lectures is to impart practical information to those who have not as yet had this experience, and I have been guided by my own recollection of those things which have generally to be explained to those who come fresh from College to take their places as Form masters in a large school. It is of great importance that these details should be understood, and carried out in practice in order to the efficient and easy working of the school machine.

I hope I shall not be considered impertinent if I conclude by expressing a hope that those who intend to go in for school work will bear in mind the immense responsibilities of the duties they propose to undertake, and the great influence for good which they can obtain over others, and that too at a time of life when the seed sown is likely to bear lasting fruit. The profession is doubtless an arduous one, but most honourable, and of absorbing interest, and one in which, more than in most, the results of hard and conscientious labour will make themselves manifest, and will cheer and reward those who endeavour honestly to do their duty.

CAMBRIDGE: PRINTED BY C. J. CLAY, M.A. AND SON, AT THE UNIVERSITY PRESS

www.ingramcontent.com/pod-product-compliance
Lightning Source LLC
Chambersburg PA
CBHW021532270326
41930CB00008B/1218